Does it soak up water?

All about absorbent and waterproof materials

Angela Royston

FRANKLIN WATTS
LONDON·SYDNEY

First published in 2009
by Franklin Watts

Copyright © Franklin Watts 2009

Franklin Watts
338 Euston Road
London NW1 3BH

Franklin Watts Australia
Level 17/207 Kent Street
Sydney, NSW 2000

Series editor: Sarah Peutrill
Art director: Jonathan Hair
Design: Elaine Wilkinson
Photographs: Paul Bricknell (unless otherwise credited)

The author and publishers would like to thank Sara Cinamon, Science
Advisor for Islington, London, for her advice with the experiments.

Picture credits: istock: pp 4l (connellyink), 18b (lepas2004), 19t (robcruse),
26t (kebuluran), 27 (hdoggrafix); Shutterstock: 4r and title page (Carolyn
Brule), 5 (Lora Clark), 8tl (ultimathule), 8tr (adv), 8b (Mika Heittola), 9t
(pixelman), 10 (LisaMarie73), 11b (Dewitt), 14 (Maxim Kazitov), 15l (Olga
Kushcheva), 15r (Eric Gevaert), 16t and title page (J. Helgason), 16b (Mindy
w.m. Chung), 17t (Joanne Harris and Daniel Bubnich), 18t (Elena Talberg), 22
(Dewitt), 23t (Michael Stokes), 23b (The Labor Shed), 24t (Dagmar
Schneider), 24b (Joe Gough), 25t (Bertie Coetzee), 26b (Kheng Guan Toh);
Wishlist Images: 6, 7, 19.
Cover images: Shutterstock tl (Lowe Llaguno), tm (LisaMarie73), tr (Kheng
Guan Toh), b (Trapdoor Media)

With thanks to our models: Conah Caple, Mary Conquest, Katie Lloyd,
Chris Penny, Darnell Smith.

Dewey number: 620.1'12

ISBN 978 0 7496 8719 9

Printed in China

Franklin Watts is a division of Hachette Children's Books,
an Hachette UK company.

www.hachette.co.uk

Please note: The investigations in this book have been thoroughly checked
and tested. We regret that the Author and Publisher cannot be held
responsible for any accidents or injury incurred while following them.

Contents

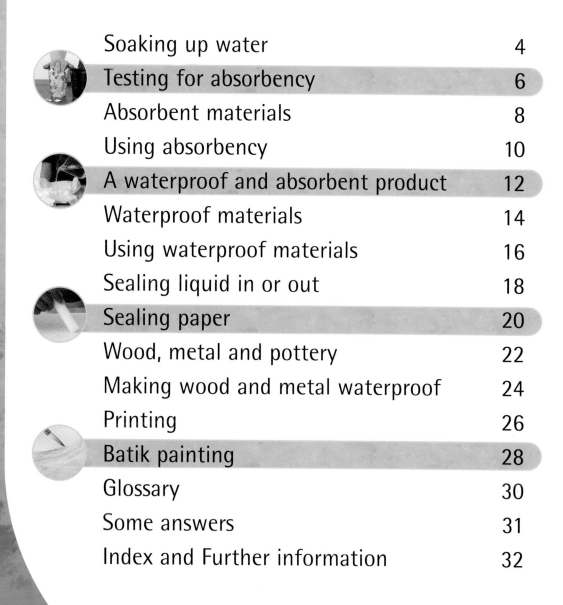

The topics highlighted above are investigations you can try.

Words in bold are in the glossary on page 30.

Soaking up water

Some things soak up water and other liquids. **Materials** that soak up liquids are said to be **absorbent**. Other materials are said to be **waterproof** or **water resistant** because they do not take in liquids at all. A third group of materials are in-between.

Some of this boy's clothes are waterproof. Which are they? What else could he use to keep dry in the rain?

Kitchen sponges quickly mop up spilt drinks and other liquids.

Soaking up liquids

You can use many different things to soak up liquids. For example, sponges are good for mopping up spills. A sponge has lots of holes, which are full of air. When you put the sponge over a spill and squeeze it, you squeeze out some of the air. When you stop squeezing and let go, the liquid rushes into the spaces left by air.

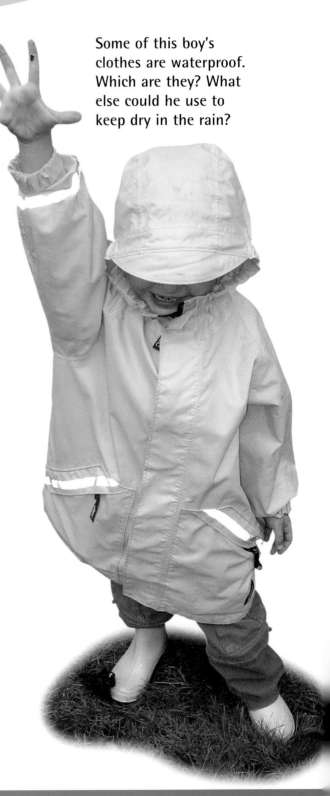

Keeping water out

Some kinds of plastic are good at keeping water out. Wellington boots keep your feet dry in the rain because the water cannot get through them. The water runs off instead.

Materials like wood and pottery do not keep water out as well as plastic does, but they do not soak up a lot of water either.

Wood does not soak up water, but it is not waterproof either. It is in-between.

Testing for absorbency

Which material would make a good covering for the floor of a hamster's cage? A material that absorbs spilt water would work well. Test these materials to see which is the most absorbent. Fill the cups to the same level to make it a fair test.

You will need:

3 clear plastic cups, potting compost, sawdust, newspaper torn into little bits, porridge oats, rice, kitchen scales, measuring jug, water, a plastic spoon.

Fill one cup with **potting compost**, one with sawdust, and one with torn-up newspaper. Pack the newspaper tightly.

1

Weigh each of the cups and write down their weight.

2

6

Slowly pour a little water into the cup of compost. Stir it and tilt the cup to see if all the water has been absorbed. Add more water and test again. Carry on until the compost is **saturated** and so cannot absorb more water. Do the same with the other cups.

Weigh each cup again and write down the weight. Subtract the dry weight from the saturated weight to see how much water each one absorbed. Which material absorbed the most?

What do you think?

Try the experiment again using porridge oats and uncooked grains of rice. Which do you think will be most absorbent? Test them and see.

Absorbent materials

Absorbent materials take in and hold water and other liquids. They can do this because they have tiny spaces that become filled with liquid. The holes in sponges are easy to see. Many fabrics, such as cotton and wool, are also

This natural sponge is the remains of a sea animal.

absorbent. They are made of **yarn** that is woven or knitted. The yarn has tiny holes, called **pores**.

Synthetic sponges are made in different shapes and colours.

Cotton T-shirts are good for a sunny day because they absorb sweat.

Paper

Some kinds of paper are more absorbent than others. Paper is made from wood that is mashed and mixed with water to make a mushy **pulp**. The pulp is spread into a thin layer to dry. It dries into a sheet of paper. However, when paper becomes wet it becomes mushy again and tears very easily.

Paper towels absorb liquids easily.

Leave some dried beans to soak in water overnight. Next day are they hard or soft? What will happen when they are cooked?

Dried food

Some materials swell up and become larger as they soak up liquid. Fresh beans and peas are dried to **preserve** them, because dried foods last a long time without going bad. Dried beans and peas have to be soaked for several hours before they are cooked. As they slowly take in the water, they swell.

Using absorbency

Absorbent materials are useful for many things. For example, washing and drying often involves absorbent materials. Mops absorb water and are used to clean floors. Bath towels and hand towels make you dry because they soak up water from your skin and hair.

Washing clothes

Most fabrics are absorbent. They could not be washed if they were not. For example, when a jumper is put into soapy water to wash it, the yarn absorbs the water. As the water is squeezed out, it brings the dirt out with it. Rinsing the jumper in clean water gets rid of the soap.

When you rub wet hair or skin with a towel, the towel absorbs the water. You get dry and the towel becomes wet!

Half fill a bowl with cool water. Put in a thick woollen jersey and squeeze it. What happens to the water?

Soil

Soil absorbs water and stores it, but different soils absorb different amounts of water. Most plants grow best in soil that absorbs some water, but not too much. For example, clay absorbs a lot of water and so, if it rains heavily, it quickly becomes too wet. Sandy soil is much lighter. However, rainwater can drain through it too fast. The best soil is in-between.

Plants grow by taking in water that has been absorbed by soil.

A waterproof and absorbent product

You will need:

2 unused baby's disposable nappies, a jug of water, old newspaper, scissors.

A baby's nappy is designed to be super absorbent and waterproof at the same time! It includes powdery grains that can absorb lots of liquid. One way to find out how something works is to take it apart and examine it.

Open up the nappy and pull off the inner lining. You may have to cut into the nappy to get under the lining. Put the lining on the newspaper.

Take off the soft wadding. Can you feel powdery grains with your fingers? Lay it alongside the inner lining and the outer plastic layer.

1

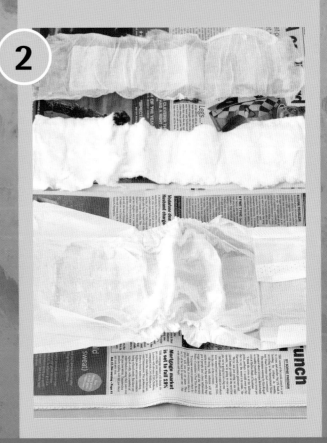

2

Pour a little water onto the inner lining, the wadding and the outer layer. Check the newspaper underneath each. What do you notice?

Which part of the nappy is absorbent? Which part is waterproof?

3

4

How much will it absorb?

Use another clean nappy.
Fill the jug with 500 ml of water.
Pour about 100 ml of the water onto the nappy. Is the inner lining wet or dry? Pour more water onto the nappy. How much can it absorb?

Waterproof materials

Something is waterproof when there are no gaps or little holes in its surface for water to get in through. Plastic, rubber and glass are all waterproof, but they are different in other ways. Rubber is bendy, while glass is rigid. Some plastics are bendy and some are rigid.

Plastic

Plastic is a synthetic material that is made from oil. Oil forms in the ground between layers of rock. Some synthetic materials are waterproof and some are absorbent.

This umbrella is made from waterproof plastic, which is synthetic.

Glass

Glass is both waterproof and **transparent**. It is the best material for windows, because it keeps rain out and lets light in. Glass is also used to make bottles, jars and other things that hold liquids.

This vase is made of transparent glass. Glass is also waterproof.

Rubber tyres are airtight and waterproof.

Rubber

Rubber is a natural material. It comes from the thick, white **sap** of rubber trees. Rubber is waterproof, flexible and hardwearing, which is why tyres for cars, lorries and other vehicles are made of it. Tyres are filled with air to provide a soft cushion between the vehicle and the road.

Using waterproof materials

Waterproof materials are used wherever water needs to be kept in or out. For example, tents and **tarpaulins** are made of tough waterproof materials to keep the rain out. Garden ponds have a thick plastic lining to keep the water in.

If you own a tent be careful not to damage it. Otherwise it might leak!

Roofing materials

Roofs are needed to keep our homes dry. Flat roofs are made of **concrete** or covered with **asphalt**, which is waterproof. Sloping roofs are usually covered with waterproof slates or tiles. Some slates are made from a kind of stone called slate. The stone is split into thin, rectangular slices. Other tiles are made of synthetic materials.

Slates and tiles are laid so that they slightly overlap. Rain runs straight off them.

Boats

Boats need to be completely watertight. Large ships are made of steel. Many small boats and yachts are made of waterproof **fibreglass**. Fibreglass is a mixture of plastic and fine threads of glass. It is strong but light in weight.

This boat has a plastic cover to keep out rain and spray.

Ask an adult to help you dig a hole in a flowerbed. Line the hole with a plastic bag and fill it with water. Now you have a mini pond! You can grow duckweed in it, or float paper boats.

Sealing liquid in or out

Water leaks through gaps or holes. Many things have a waterproof seal around them to stop this happening. For example, the doorway of a washing machine has a rubber seal that fits tightly to the door. If it didn't, water would leak onto the floor.

Sealed tops

The tops of bottles and pots are often sealed, too. For example, yoghurt tops are waterproof so they do not absorb the yoghurt, and they are glued to the rim of the pot. The glue is waterproof so that the yoghurt does not leak out. Look for waterproof seals, too, between the tiles in a bathroom and between the hand basin and the wall.

Sealing absorbent materials

Liquids, such as milk and juice, are sometimes packaged in cardboard cartons. Cardboard and paper are absorbent so the cartons have to be sealed. Some are covered with plastic or metal foil, and some are waxed.

Milk or juice is often sold in waxed cardboard cartons.

Examine a drinks carton. How has it been treated to make it waterproof? You may need to ask an adult to help you cut open the carton.

19

Sealing paper

Writing paper is slightly
absorbent but it can be made
waterproof. Test different materials
on sheets of paper to see which materials make
a good waterproof seal. Leave one piece of paper
unsealed so that you can compare the others with it.

You will need:

5 small sheets of paper,
a candle, petroleum jelly,
cooking oil, PVA glue, food colouring,
measuring jug half-filled with water,
old newspaper.

Rub one of the sheets with the
candle until it feels waxy all over.

1

Rub another sheet of paper with
petroleum jelly, and another with
cooking oil. Spread PVA glue over
the fourth sheet of paper and let it
dry. Leave the last sheet as it is.

2

Lay a sheet of the paper on some old newspaper. Add some food colouring to the jug of water. Pour a little of the coloured water onto one of the five sheets.

Roll the drops of water around. Will they run off? Do the same with the other sheets. To make the test fair, drop the same amount of water on each sheet.

What happens?

What do you think will happen when you dip the end of each sheet of paper into the coloured water? Test your prediction. Are both sides of the paper sealed?

Wood, metal and pottery

Most materials are not waterproof. When they get wet, they take in a little water but then dry out. With bricks and many materials, this is not a problem. However, wood rots and iron and steel **rust** if they are often wet or damp.

Rotting

Fungi make wood rot. Fungi are **microbes** but they are a bit like plants. Fungi need water and food to survive and to grow. They feed on the wood and gradually break it down. You can see rotting wood in forests, where trees or tree branches have fallen down.

This fallen tree is rotting.

Rusting

Both iron and steel rust.

Iron and steel rust when they are in contact with water or damp air. The surface of the metal turns brownish-red. The metal becomes weaker and begins to crumble. Rusting is also called **corrosion**.

Pottery

Pottery is made from clay. If it is untreated, it slowly absorbs water, but it does not rot or rust. Pottery is usually covered with a layer of **glaze**. The glaze is slightly shiny and it makes the pottery waterproof.

This flower pot is made of unglazed pottery. Can you see where it has absorbed some water?

Making wood and metal waterproof

Wooden doors, window frames and furniture are usually painted, varnished or polished to protect them from rotting. Metal gates and railings are painted to stop them from rusting. Metal can also be protected by covering it with a thin layer of metal **chrome**. Chrome-plating is silvery and very shiny. It is used on taps.

Paint

Gloss paint or enamel paint are best for protecting wood from rotting. They contain an oil or resin, which forms a waterproof seal as the paint dries. The paint also contains **pigment** to colour it and a liquid that keeps the paint runny until it is used. Once a surface has been painted, the liquid **evaporates** and the paint dries.

Paint protects metal (left) and wood (above).

Varnish dries to form a watertight skin, like paint does. It is often used to protect wood.

Oil

Metal can also be oiled to protect it from rusting. Oil does not mix with water and so a thin layer of oil or grease keeps water out. For example, bike chains can be coated with oil to stop them from rusting.

Pour a little cooking oil into a clear plastic cup of water. What happens? Stir it up and leave it for a few minutes. What happens to the oil and water?

Printing

Some methods of printing use the fact that oil or wax don't mix with water. **Batik** is a way of dyeing cloth to give a pattern. **Offset litho** is a way of printing words and pictures.

Batik

Batik is a **traditional** way of dyeing cloth used in Indonesia and other countries. Parts of the cloth are covered with melted wax. The cloth absorbs the wax. When the cloth is dipped into water containing dye, the areas covered by the wax do not absorb the dye. When the wax is removed, the fabric below is still the original colour. The process can be repeated to give several different colours.

In batik, hot wax is brushed or spread over parts of the cloth (above). The cloth is then dyed and dried (right).

Offset litho

In offset litho, words and pictures are transferred to a printing plate, which is usually made of metal or plastic. The parts of the plate that are covered by letters or a picture change so that they are able to absorb oil. The whole plate is covered with oily printing ink and then washed. The oily ink sticks only to the words and pictures. The plate is then ready to print.

Printed sheets roll off an offset litho machine.

Batik painting

You can use the method of producing batik to make a batik painting on paper. It uses candle wax to stop paint reaching some parts of the paper.

Use the candle to draw on the paper. Press hard and work slowly. You can either draw a picture or a pattern.

Cover the paper with watercolour paint. Paint over the wax as well as the unwaxed paper.

1

2

The candle wax will not take in the paint. Can you see the drawing you did with the candle through the paint?

3

Draw another picture with the candle. This time, use different colours of paint in different parts of the picture. The wax will stop them running into each other.

4

Keeping it a secret

Try using a candle to write a secret message to a friend. They will have to paint the sheet to see the message.

Glossary

absorbent   Able to soak up liquid.

asphalt   A material that is waterproof and looks like tar.

batik   A method of dyeing fabric in which wax is used to protect part of the fabric from the dye.

chrome   A kind of metal that does not rust.

concrete   A strong, hard building material made from sand, gravel, cement and water.

corrosion   Rusting or similar process that eats something away.

evaporates   Changes from a liquid into a gas.

fibreglass   A material that is a mixture of plastic and strands of glass.

fungi   A group of living things. Mushrooms and moulds are kinds of fungi.

glaze   A smooth, shiny coating.

material   The substance that something is made of.

microbe   A very small living thing.

offset litho   A method of printing in which part of the printing plate is changed so that it absorbs oil.

pigment   A powdered solid used in paint to give it a colour.

pores   Tiny holes.

potting compost   A mixture of decayed leaves and other plant remains that is used to make soil better for growing plants.

preserve   Keep from rotting or other kind of damage.

pulp   A mushy wet mixture.

rust   A reddish-brown coating that forms on iron and steel when it is in contact with water and air.

sap   Plant juice.

saturated   When something has absorbed so much liquid it can hold no more.

synthetic material   A material made from oil, coal or other material.

tarpaulin   A large, tough waterproof fabric sheet.

traditional   Something, such as a process or skill, that is handed down through the generations.

transparent   See-through.

waterproof   Unable to absorb water.

water resistant   Waterproof.

yarn   A thread – a fine cord of twisted fibres (such as cotton, silk or wool) used in sewing and weaving.

Some answers

Page 4: He could also hold an umbrella to keep off the rain.

Page 7: It is likely that the newspaper absorbs the most water and the sawdust the least, but exactly how much water each material absorbs depends on how tightly packed it is.

The porridge oats absorb more water than the uncooked grains of rice. They are softer and so water can get into them more easily.

Page 9: The beans will become soft when they are cooked.

Page 11: The woollen jersey soaks up most or all of the water.

Page 13: You should have found that the wadding is absorbent and the outer layer is waterproof. The lining lets water through but does not absorb it.

Nappies vary in how much water they can absorb. Nappies for larger babies and toddlers will absorb more than those for small babies.

Page 19: Many cartons are covered with a film of metal foil inside to make them waterproof. Others are waxed.

Page 21: All of the materials seal the paper so that the water rolls around instead of being absorbed. The PVA glue, however, makes the best seal.

When you dip the sheets of paper into the jug of coloured water, you should find that only the sheet that is covered with oil does not absorb any water. This is because the oil has soaked through the paper sealing both sides of the paper.

Page 25: When oil and water are mixed together, the oil always separates and floats to the surface.

Index

Further information

www.bbc.co.uk/schools/ks2bitesize/science/
materials.shtml
Activities and quiz about materials.

www.sciencekids.co.nz/gamesactivities/
materialproperties.html
Allows you to test whether various materials
are waterproof. This New Zealand site also
includes experiments and facts as well as
games and activities.

http://computer.howstuffworks.com/
offset-printing2.htm
Explains how offset printing works.

www.sciencenewsforkids.org/articles/20030305
/Note2.asp
Find out about a new waterproof material that
scientists are developing using technology based
on butterfly wings. You can also find out about
other science news stories.

www.batikguild.org.uk/whatisbatik.as
Tells you more about the art of batik.

Note to parents and teachers: Every effort has been made by the
Publishers to ensure that these websites are suitable for children,
that they are of the highest educational value, and that they contain
no inappropriate or offensive material. However, because of the nature
of the Internet, it is impossible to guarantee that the contents of these
sites will not be altered. We strongly advise that Internet access is
supervised by a responsible adult.